THE POWER OF SELF-LOVE

Reclaim Your Worth, Heal Your Heart,
and get your intuitive intelligence at work

THE POWER OF SELF-LOVE

Reclaim Your Worth, Heal Your Heart, and get your intuitive intelligence at work

PREETI KAPOOR

REALITY SHAPING MENTOR

Available on amazonkindle

Worldwide Published by

Pendown Press

PREMIUM BUSINESS PUBLISHER

PENDOWN PRESS LLP

An ISO 9001 & ISO 14001 Certified Co.,

Regd. Office: 3767A, Kanhaiya Nagar,
Tri Nagar, Delhi-110035
Ph.: 8130886000, 9650072927, 8595249536
E-mail: info@pendownpress.com
Branch Office: 1A/2A, 20, Hari Sadan, Ansari Road,
Daryaganj, New Delhi-110002
Ph.: 011-45794768
Website: PendownPress.com

Edition: 2025
Price: ₹ 299
ISBN:978-93-6338-691-4

Layout and Cover Designed by Pendown Graphics Team
Printed and Bound in India by Thomson Press India Ltd.

To every soul who's ever doubted their worth—

May this book be a gentle reminder that you are enough, just as you are.

To the warriors healing silently and choosing love daily, this is for you.

With all my heart, I dedicate this journey to you.

TABLE OF CONTENTS

ACKNOWLEDGMENTS

Whatever I have achieved in life would not have been possible without the unwavering support of my husband, Anshul Kapoor. You've stood beside me through every step of this journey, carrying our shared responsibilities with grace, strength, and love. Thank you from the depths of my heart for being my rock, my encouragement, and the constant reminder to live up to my fullest potential.

To my children Bharavi & Udaya, you are my greatest source of joy and inspiration. Thank you for being my teachers, for showing me the true essence of life through your eyes and hearts. You bring meaning to every moment.

To my parents, my foundation, my roots. The wings I soar with today were gifted by your love, sacrifices, and the values you instilled in me. I carry you with me in everything I do.

To my siblings, and especially my sister Riddhi, my biggest cheerleader, your faith in me has been a guiding light. To my dearest friends and confidants, thank you for teaching me the power of self-love. Somyak reminded me to always be unapologetically myself — 'You do you, Preeti!' — and Ajeet taught me the art of being present and cherishing life's simple, fleeting moments.

A heartfelt thank you to Dinesh Verma and the incredible team at Pendown Press. From the birth of an idea to the birth of this book, your guidance, professionalism, and passion made it all possible.

Lastly, to every soul who has been part of my journey, whether named or unnamed, know that your love, support, and belief in me have been felt deeply. You each hold a permanent and special place in my heart.

This journey would not have been possible without you all. Thank you for giving me the courage to move forward with confidence and clarity.

PREFACE

There comes a moment in life when all the noise fades and you're left facing one question: Do I truly love myself, or have I just been surviving?

For me, that moment came quietly but powerfully. I had spent years trying to be "enough" in every possible way, for work, for people, for society. From the outside, it looked fine. But inside, I felt disconnected from the one person I had never fully embraced—myself.

I didn't write this book because I had all the answers—I wrote it because I was searching for them too. There was a time when I constantly looked outside myself for validation, approval, and love. I wore masks, played roles, and silenced my own voice just to fit in. And yet, I felt empty. It wasn't until I turned inward that things began to shift.

That's when this journey began.

This book isn't just filled with ideas. It's filled with lived truths, personal insights, and the gentle tools that helped me reconnect with my heart. I didn't want this to feel like another "fix-yourself" manual. I wanted it to feel like a warm, steady hand on your shoulder. Because self-love isn't a goal you tick off; it's a way of being, one that unfolds slowly and beautifully over time.

Inside these pages, you'll find more than affirmations and exercises. You'll find emotional honesty, permission to rest, and the courage to be real. You'll learn how to protect your peace, forgive your past, and show up for yourself—over and over again.

I wrote this for the version of me who needed it the most. And maybe that version lives in you too.

So, take your time. Go gently. This isn't just a book. It's a homecoming.

With all my love,

Preeti Kapoor

Why This Book

I wrote this book because self-love is something many of us talk about but rarely understand deeply. For years, I searched for it in achievements, people, and perfection—only to realize it had to come from within. This book is my honest attempt to simplify that journey for you. It's not about being flawless; it's about being kind to yourself in the mess, the growth, and the in-betweens. I've combined personal reflections, gentle practices, and real-life tools that helped me reconnect with myself. Whether you're starting from scratch or rebuilding after heartbreak, this book offers you a space to pause, heal, and remember your worth. I hope it becomes a soft place for you to land—again and again.

INTRODUCTION

Read this like a letter from your future self...

Hey you,

Yes, you—with a loud mind and a tired heart. You've done so much for everyone else. You've chased goals, ticked boxes, and smiled even on heavy days. But have you paused... and asked yourself, "What about me?"

This book isn't just about self-love. It's a mirror. One that doesn't distort, doesn't judge, and doesn't care if your hair's messy or your plans are too.

Inside these pages, you won't find someone telling you what to do—you'll find someone reminding you of what you already know. That your value isn't tied to your productivity. Those boundaries aren't selfish. That resting is not quitting. That your softness is your strength.

This isn't your typical self-help guide. It's a warm cup of chai on a stormy day. It's a nudge. A hug. A gentle voice saying—you're allowed to love yourself, wildly and without apology.

Let's begin. You're ready—even if you don't feel like it yet.

1
Chapter

Understanding Your Relationship with Yourself

"You yourself, as much as anybody in the entire universe, deserve your love and affection."

~ Buddha

Objective:

This chapter helps you understand how you see yourself, identify emotional blockages, and build a positive relationship with yourself.

Introduction: The Foundation of Every Other Relationship

The most important connection you'll ever build is the one within. Before you can form strong, healthy bonds with others, it's essential to develop a positive inner relationship. The way you view and treat yourself influences everything—your personal relationships, career, health, and overall happiness.

Yet, this inner bond is often the most neglected. We spend so much time meeting others' needs and chasing their approval that we overlook our own well-being. But how can you fully care for or connect with others if you haven't learned to care for the person in the mirror?

This chapter is about strengthening that inner connection. We'll explore ways to understand who you truly are, let go of harmful thought patterns, and start treating yourself with the love and respect that every human deserves.

How Do You See Yourself?

The way you see yourself, your self-image, plays a huge role in your life. It impacts your self-esteem, your confidence, and your ability to handle challenges. But where does your self-image come from? It doesn't come from nowhere, it's shaped by your experiences, the people around you, and even society's standards.

These inner thoughts can become a force for growth or a barrier that holds you back. If you constantly believe you're not enough, that mindset can block your potential. Negative self-talk warps reality and often leads to feelings of unworthiness and self-doubt.

How to manage self-perception for personal growth?

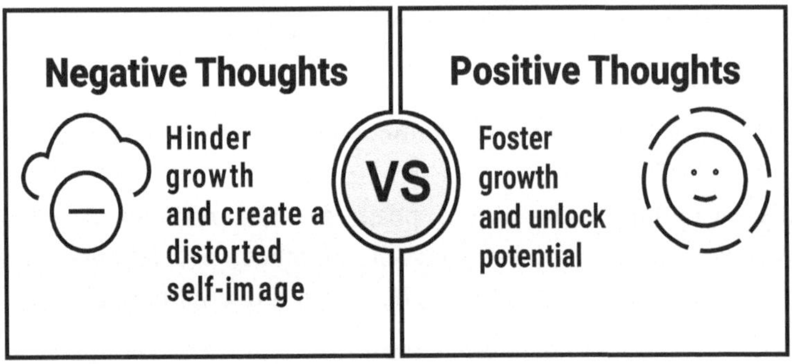

Exercise: The Mirror Test

To understand how you really feel about yourself, let's do a simple exercise. It's called the mirror test, and it's designed to show you the hidden feelings you might have about yourself.

Steps:

1. Find a mirror where you won't be interrupted.
2. Look at yourself in the mirror for two full minutes.
3. Pay attention to how you feel during these two minutes. Are you uncomfortable, proud, judgmental, accepting, or loving?
4. Ask yourself: "How do I feel when I look at myself?"
5. Notice the thoughts that come up. Are they kind, or do they make you feel bad?

This is not about vanity; it's about awareness. The way you feel when you look at yourself can tell you a lot about how you perceive your worth. Those feelings are often formed by past experiences and beliefs you may not even realize you hold.

Where Does Your Self-Image Come From?

Now that you've had a chance to think about how you feel about yourself, let's dig deeper into where these feelings come from. Our self-image is influenced by many things, from childhood experiences to societal standards to our past relationships.

1. **Childhood Experiences: The Foundation of How We See Ourselves**

   Our early experiences have a big impact on how we view ourselves. The messages we receive from our parents, teachers, and friends shape the way we see ourselves as adults.

Examples:

- A child who is always praised for being smart might grow up believing that their worth depends on being the best at everything.
- A child who is criticized for being "too emotional" may grow up hiding their feelings because they think being emotional is a flaw.
- If a child hears negative comments about their appearance, they might carry those feelings into adulthood, thinking they're not good enough.

Reflection:

Think about your childhood. Were there things people said that made you feel good or bad about yourself? Can you see how those early messages still influence the way you see yourself today?

2. **Society and Media: The Pressure to Be "Perfect"**

In addition to our childhood experiences, society also plays a big role in shaping how we view ourselves. From TV shows to social media, there's constant pressure to look a certain way or live up to certain standards. These pressures can cause us to feel insecure about ourselves, especially if we don't meet those standards.

Examples:

- The beauty standards shown in magazines and on social media can make us feel like we're not attractive if we don't look a certain way.

- Society often links success to money or status. If you don't have those things, you might feel like you've failed.
- Social media makes us compare our lives to others, which can lead to feelings of inadequacy or self-doubt.

Reflection:

How have societal pressures or media affected the way you see yourself? Are there certain standards that you've been trying to meet that might not even matter to you?

3. **Past Relationships: How They Shape Our Beliefs About Ourselves**

Our relationships with others, whether romantic, family, or friendships, can also affect how we see ourselves. If we've been in toxic relationships or faced rejection, it can leave emotional scars that shape our self-image.

Examples:

- A toxic relationship where someone constantly belittled you can leave you with feelings of unworthiness, even after the relationship ends.
- A failure at work or in a personal project can make you feel like you're not capable or good enough, even though failure is part of the learning process.
- Criticism from family, friends, or colleagues can cause lasting self-doubt.

Reflection:

Think about a past experience where you felt rejected or criticized. How did it affect the way you saw yourself? Can you see how that experience may have shaped your self-image?

Changing Negative Self-Beliefs

The good news is that your self-image can change. Once you understand where your negative beliefs come from, you can begin to replace them with healthier, more empowering beliefs.

Examples of Reframing Negative Beliefs:

Negative Thought	Reframed Thought
"I'm not good enough."	"I am constantly learning and growing. I am enough as I am."
"I'm too emotional."	"My emotions are a strength. They help me connect with others and understand myself better."
"I don't meet society's standards."	"I define my own standards. I choose what makes me happy and fulfilled."

Action Step:

Pick one negative belief you have about yourself and write it down. Then, reframe it with a positive, empowering statement. Repeat this new statement to yourself every day.

How to Talk to Yourself with Kindness

The way we talk to ourselves is a big part of our self-image. When you speak to yourself with kindness and compassion, you help heal negative thoughts and build a stronger self-esteem. You wouldn't speak to your friends the way you sometimes speak to yourself—so why do it to yourself?

Tips for Kind Self-Talk:

1. **Be Aware:** Notice how you talk to yourself, especially when you're feeling stressed or down. Is it positive or negative?
2. **Speak Kindly:** Treat yourself the way you would treat a close friend—with encouragement, patience, and understanding.
3. **Use Positive Affirmations:** Remind yourself of your strengths and worth every day. For example: "I am worthy of love and success," or "I am enough just as I am."

Exercise: The Self-Talk Journal

For the next week, write down your thoughts about yourself, especially when you're feeling down or anxious. Review your journal at the end of the week and notice any patterns. Are you being kind to yourself, or are your thoughts mostly critical? Use this journal to practice shifting to more positive, kind self-talk.

Meditation for Self-Love

Meditation can help you connect with your inner self and heal old wounds. A simple practice of self-love meditation can change how you feel about yourself.

Steps:

1. Sit in a quiet place, close your eyes, and take a few deep breaths.
2. Imagine yourself as a child—your younger self—and picture yourself holding that child with love and care.
3. Say kind things to this version of yourself: "You are loved. You are enough."
4. Let your younger self feel comforted and supported. You deserve the same love and care you give to others.

Conclusion: Starting Your Journey to Self-Love

The most important relationship in your life is the one with yourself. By becoming aware of how you see yourself, identifying old beliefs that no longer serve you, and replacing them with loving, kind thoughts, you can begin to improve your relationship with yourself.

Self-love isn't something that happens overnight—it's a journey. But with every small step, you'll get closer to building the kind of self-relationship that helps you grow, feel good about yourself, and connect with others in a meaningful way.

Final Thought:

What's one small thing you can do today to show yourself some love and kindness? Start with that, and remember that every step counts.

TIME TO THINK

1. **When you looked at yourself in the mirror during the exercise, what was the very first thought or feeling that came up and what might that say about how you truly see yourself?**

    ____

    ____

    ____

    ____

    ____

2. **Can you identify one message from your childhood, past relationships, or society that still influences your self-image today? Is it helping or hurting you?**

    ____

    ____

    ____

    ____

    ____

3. **What's one kind thing you can say to yourself today that you rarely hear—even from others? Write it down and repeat it aloud.**

    ____

    ____

    ____

    ____

    ____

2
Chapter

Releasing Limiting Beliefs

"If you don't love yourself, how in the hell you gonna love somebody else?"

~ RuPaul

Objective:

This chapter is about identifying the quiet inner scripts that hold you back—and replacing them with beliefs that support your freedom, power, and truth.

Introduction: The Invisible Walls

Most people don't fail because of external circumstances—they stop themselves before they even begin.

It happens quietly.

A thought whispers: *"That's not for people like me."*

Or: *"I'm too late."*

Or: *"Who am I to even try?"*

These are limiting beliefs. They don't scream. They hum—softly, steadily—until they become your reality.

But here's the truth: Beliefs are not facts. They are thoughts you've repeated for so long that they feel real. In this chapter, we won't just uncover these beliefs—we'll tear them out at the root and replace them with something far more powerful: possibility.

What Exactly Are Limiting Beliefs?

Limiting beliefs are internal assumptions that define what you believe is possible, permissible, or realistic for yourself. They limit your behavior, shrink your potential, and quietly shape your choices.

You'll know you're in the grip of a limiting belief when you catch yourself saying things like:

- "I'm not the kind of person who can do that."
- "It's too late for me."
- "People like me don't get opportunities like that."
- "I always mess things up."
- "I'm not meant for success."

But none of these are universal truths. They're inherited stories—picked up through culture, pain, rejection, and repetition.

Why Beliefs Matter More Than Motivation

Most people think change is about willpower. But willpower can't fight beliefs.

If you believe you're unworthy, no amount of discipline will make you feel confident.

If you believe success is for "others," you'll self-sabotage before you even start.

Beliefs are the silent architects of your life.

Until you change your blueprint, nothing outside will change permanently.

Exercise: The "Glass Ceiling" Map

Let's start by mapping your internal ceilings.

Step 1: Pick an area of your life you feel stuck in.

Examples: Career, relationships, health, money, creativity.

Step 2: Complete this sentence:

"I'd be able to make progress in this area if only I weren't so ________."

Fill in the blank. Maybe you say "lazy," "emotional," "old," "unqualified," etc.

Now ask yourself:

"Who taught me that being ________ was a flaw?"

"What evidence do I have that proves this belief is universally true?"

Often, you'll realize you're living by someone else's rulebook—one that was never even yours to begin with.

The Science of Belief Formation

From a neurological point of view, beliefs are mental shortcuts formed by repetition. Your brain creates a story to make sense of the world, and then files that story under "truth."

But here's the twist: The brain doesn't care if the belief is helpful—it only cares if it's familiar. Which is why unhealthy beliefs feel "safe," and unfamiliar ones (like "I deserve better") feel like lies at first.

To change a belief, you don't need to "fix yourself." You just need to offer your brain a new narrative—and repeat it until it becomes the dominant script.

The 3 Faces of Limiting Beliefs

Most limiting beliefs fall into one of these three categories:

1. **Identity Beliefs**

   "This is just who I am."

   These define your sense of self—often based on past versions of you.

   Examples:

   - "I'm not a people person."
   - "I'm bad with money."
   - "I'm not creative."

   Reframe: Who says identity is fixed? You're allowed to evolve.

2. **Capability Beliefs**

   "I can't do this."

   These limit what you think you're able to learn or achieve.

   Examples:

   - "I'm not tech-savvy."
   - "I could never run a business."
   - "I'm too shy to lead."

   Reframe: Replace with "I'm not skilled... yet."

3. **Deservability Beliefs**

   "I don't deserve this."

   These are rooted in shame, guilt, or trauma.

   Examples:

   - "I've made too many mistakes."
   - "Others need it more than me."
   - "I haven't earned happiness."

Reframe: You don't earn worthiness—you were born with it.

Tool: "Belief Loop Breaker"

Beliefs create behaviors. Behaviors create results. Results reinforce beliefs.

Here's how to break the loop:

Current Loop	New Loop
Belief: I always fail →	**Belief:** I'm learning faster each time
Behavior: Don't try →	**Behavior:** Take one small risk
Result: Nothing improves →	**Result:** Tiny progress builds belief

Start small. One change in the loop changes the entire direction.

The Language of Limitation

Language exposes belief. Catch yourself using phrases like:

- "I'm just not the type of person who..."
- "I should..."
- "I always mess up..."
- "That's just the way it is..."

These are red flags. Replace them with:

- "I'm exploring what's possible for me."
- "I'm becoming the kind of person who..."
- "I'm learning new ways to handle this."

Rewrite Your Narrative

Let's change the belief not by debating it—but by rewriting it.

Exercise: "Rewrite the Scene"

Pick a moment in your life where a limiting belief was born. Now, reimagine that moment with one difference: **You speak up for yourself.**

Imagine telling the teacher, the parent, the partner, or the voice in your head:

"You're wrong about me. I know who I am."

Write it like a movie scene.

Make it powerful.

Reclaim that voice.

This is not fantasy—it's reprogramming.

Visualization: Future You, Liberated

Visualize a version of you **three years from now** who:

- Has fully released limiting beliefs.
- Lives confidently, makes bold decisions, and embraces failure as part of growth.

Now answer:

- What habits does this version of you have?
- What people do this version keep close to?
- What limiting belief does this version not even remember anymore?

Now work backward: What would this future version of you tell you to do today?

This creates an emotional bridge between now and the future—your brain starts acting "as if" you are already becoming that version.

Upgrade Script

Create a personal affirmation based on the exact belief you want to release.

Old belief: "I'm too much."

Upgrade: "I am deep, passionate, and full of light—and I attract people who see my fire as a gift."

Write it. Say it. Own it.

It's not cheesy. It's neurological.

The Subtle Beliefs You Didn't Know You Had

Some limiting beliefs are loud, but many are in disguise. They masquerade as common sense or maturity. Examples:

- "It's better to stay quiet than cause conflict." (You may fear rejection.)
- "It's selfish to prioritize my needs." (You may fear being seen as 'bad'.)
- "If I don't do it perfectly, it's not worth doing." (You may fear failure.)

Ask yourself:

"What thoughts sound responsible on the surface but are actually holding me back?"

Write them down. Trace their emotional cost. These beliefs are dangerous because they sound reasonable. But they keep you small.

The Role of Environment

Beliefs don't live in isolation—they're fed by your environment.

- Are you surrounded by people who challenge you or people who doubt everything?
- Do your surroundings reflect who you're becoming—or who you've been?
- Are you exposing yourself to voices, content, and spaces that build you up?

Just like a plant needs good soil, your mindset needs supportive surroundings. You don't rise in toxic soil. Curate your ecosystem.

Pattern Interruption Technique

Each time a limiting thought shows up, interrupt it with one of these actions:

1. Physically move: Stand up, shake your body, jump once. Change your state.
2. Say "Stop" out loud: Disrupt the cycle.
3. Replace the thought immediately with a truth-based counterstatement.

Example:

- **Limiting belief:** "Nobody cares what I say."
- **Interruption:** *Stand up*, say "*Stop*," replace with:

"My voice has value, and the right people are listening."

Doing this repeatedly rewires your brain's default loop.

Daily Challenge: The 10-Day "Belief Flip"

For the next 10 days:

1. Notice one limiting thought per day.

2. Write it down.
3. Flip it into an empowering statement.
4. Speak it out loud. (Yes, out loud.)

Example:

- Thought: "Nobody listens to me."
- Flip: "My voice carries value. I speak with clarity and presence."

Final Thought: Beliefs Are Choices in Disguise

Beliefs are not final. They are not fate. They are just decisions you've been making—on repeat.

The good news?

You can choose again.

You can choose better.

You can choose now.

TIME TO THINK

1. **What is one negative thought I often say to myself, and where do I think it came from?**

2. **"What kind of life is waiting for me on the other side of that belief?"**

3. **If a close friend had this same belief, what would I lovingly tell them?**

3
Chapter

Developing a Self-Love Mindset

"As I began to love myself, I freed myself of anything that is not good for my health—food, people, things, situations."

~ Charlie Chaplin

Cultivating Self-Compassion, Gratitude & Emotional Resilience

Self-love is not arrogance, vanity, or selfishness. It is the quiet strength of knowing you are worthy, even when the world forgets to tell you. It is choosing to show up for yourself again and again—not because you are perfect, but because you are human.

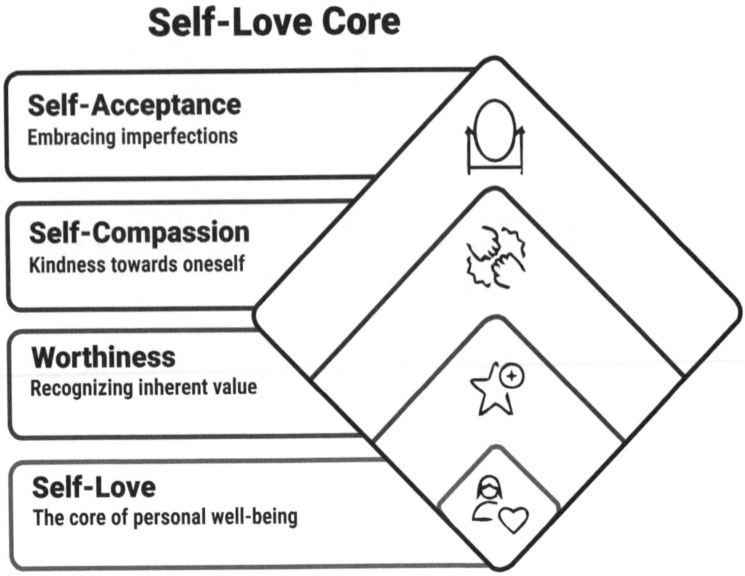

This chapter is your gentle guide to building that mindset; one that supports, soothes, uplifts, and believes in you. It starts not with a big change, but with a soft whisper:

"I matter. My needs matter. I am enough."

Let's explore how to nurture this powerful inner foundation through self-compassion, gratitude, boundaries, and emotional healing.

1. What Is Self-Compassion?

Imagine your closest friend going through a tough time. You wouldn't insult them, shame them, or tell them they're weak. You'd probably say, "It's okay. You did your best. You'll get through this."

Now ask yourself honestly:

Do you treat yourself the same way?

Self-compassion means showing yourself the same level of kindness, patience, and understanding that you would show to someone you love.

It is the warm hug when your heart breaks.

The soft voice that says, *"Try again."*

The pause that allows you to rest without guilt.

Self-compassion is not about avoiding responsibility; it's about **choosing healing over harshness.**

2. How to Practice Self-Compassion Every Day

The way we talk to ourselves in private shapes how we feel in public. That inner voice matters. It becomes the lens through which we see the world.

Here are small, meaningful ways to build self-compassion into your daily life:

Speak Kindly to Yourself

Replace criticism with care.

Instead of: "I'm so lazy."

Say: "I needed rest. I'll begin again now."

Your words can either be your wounds or your wings.

Forgive Yourself

We all carry mistakes, regrets, and past decisions. But punishment is not the same as growth.

Remind yourself: *"I did the best I could with what I knew then."*

Forgiveness is a bridge between your past and your future.

Rest Without Guilt

You don't have to earn your rest.

You don't have to be productive 24/7.

Sometimes the bravest thing you can do is pause, breathe, and simply be.

Accept Yourself

Acceptance doesn't mean you stop evolving.

It means you stop fighting yourself while you grow.

Say: "This is who I am today, and I still choose to love myself."

3. Cultivating Gratitude for Yourself

Gratitude isn't just about thanking the world; it's about thanking yourself, too.

Think about this: Your heart beats every second. You breathe without asking. You've made it through every hard day so far. Isn't that something to appreciate?

Gratitude is the act of seeing beauty in your journey even the messy parts.

Morning Gratitude Ritual (Exercise)

Start each day with a quiet moment. Write down:

- Five things you love or appreciate about yourself.
- One thing you're proud of from yesterday.
- A personal quality that helped you survive hard times.

This daily reminder builds your inner light. Over time, you'll stop searching for validation outside—you'll already feel it inside.

Self-Gratitude Journal

Set aside a small notebook. Use it only for appreciating yourself.

Write about:

- Times you showed courage.
- Days you made someone smile.
- Skills you've learned.
- Emotions you faced with honesty.

It becomes a book of evidence—proof that you are worthy, always.

4. Understanding Boundaries: The Invisible Shield of Self-Love

Boundaries are not walls; they are bridges of respect—both for yourself and others.

They help you protect your peace, your energy, and your emotional space.

Without boundaries, resentment builds.

With boundaries, clarity grows.

What Kind of Boundaries Do You Need?

- **Emotional:** Protect your feelings from being manipulated.

  "I will not accept being spoken to in that tone."

- **Physical:** Respect your body, space, and rest.

  "I need time alone after work to recharge."

- **Mental:** Guard your focus and beliefs.

  "I choose not to engage in gossip or negativity."

Boundary Setting Exercise

Take a journal and write:

1. Three situations where you often feel drained, resentful, or disrespected.

2. What boundary could you create to protect your energy in each situation?
3. Practice simple "No" statements, like:
   - "No, I can't help today."
   - "No, that doesn't feel right to me."
   - "No, thank you."

Remember: Saying "no" to others is often a yes to yourself.

You don't need to explain your boundaries to everyone.

You only need to honor them.

5. Creating Your Personal Self-Love Declaration

A Self-Love Declaration is like your soul's signature.

It's a reminder of who you are—when you forget.

Exercise: Write Your Self-Love Declaration

Take a few deep breaths. Put your hand on your heart. Then write:

"I choose to love and accept myself as I am.

I am allowed to grow, heal, and evolve at my own pace.

I release self-doubt and embrace my truth.

My worth is not up for debate—I am enough."

Now, read it aloud every morning. Let the words sink in.

Let them become your truth.

If you ever feel lost, return to this declaration. It is your inner compass.

6. Daily Affirmations for Self-Love

Affirmations are more than words; they are seeds planted in your subconscious.

With consistency, they bloom into belief.

Here are a few to repeat daily:

- "I am enough just as I am."
- "I honor my needs and take care of myself."
- "I deserve love, peace, and joy."
- "My feelings are valid, and my voice matters."
- "I release comparison and trust my path."
- "I forgive myself and choose progress over perfection."

Stand in front of the mirror. Look into your own eyes.

Say these out loud. Say them until they feel real.

Because what you speak to yourself, you become.

7. Emotional Resilience: Bouncing Back With Self-Love

Life doesn't promise ease. There will be pain, loss, and failure.

But with self-love, you become resilient—not because life gets easier, but because you get stronger.

When challenges come:

- Breathe through them.
- Allow your feelings to be felt—without judgment.
- Remind yourself: *"This is hard, but I am safe. I am growing through this."*

Emotional resilience is not about "being positive all the time."

It's about being compassionate even when you're not okay.

Final Thoughts: You Are Your Own Home

This chapter is not a checklist; it's a path.

A journey of coming home to yourself.

Of meeting your flaws with kindness.

Of turning pain into power.

Of finally realizing—you've always been worthy of love, especially from yourself.

The world outside can only reflect what you believe inside.

So build a love that is unshakable, unconditional, and rooted in truth.

"The most powerful relationship you'll ever have is the one you build with yourself."

Time To Think

1. **When was the last time I truly showed kindness or forgiveness to myself and what did it feel like?**

    ____

    ____

    ____

    ____

    ____

2. **What are three things I genuinely appreciate about myself today, even if no one else notices them?**

    ____

    ____

    ____

    ____

    ____

3. **Where in my life do I need to set a boundary and what's one loving way I can express it?**

    ____

    ____

    ____

    ____

    ____

4
Chapter

The Power of Self-Love

"Owning our story and loving ourselves through that process is the bravest thing that we'll ever do."

~ Brené Brown

Objective:

Understanding self-love and building a personalized routine that helps you feel mentally, emotionally, physically, and spiritually balanced.

What is Self-Love?

Self-love is not about expensive spa days or luxury vacations. It's about taking small, consistent actions to take care of your well-being. It means giving yourself permission to pause, breathe, and listen to your body and mind.

It's a gentle reminder: "I matter too."

Let's understand the four key areas of self-love in a very simple way:

1. Physical Self-Love

This is how you care for your body, the vehicle that carries you through life. When your body feels good, your mind and emotions also feel better.

Simple ways to practice physical self-love:

- Eat meals that nourish you, not just fill you.
- Sleep for at least 7-8 hours.
- Stretch, walk, or dance for 20–30 minutes daily.
- Drink enough water.
- Give yourself rest without guilt.

Even taking a short nap when you're tired is an act of self-love.

2. Emotional Self-Love

This is about allowing your feelings without judgment. It's okay to cry. It's okay to feel overwhelmed. Emotional self-love is creating space for your feelings and responding to them kindly.

Ways to practice emotional self-love:

- Write in a journal when you're feeling heavy.
- Say no to things that drain your energy.
- Speak to a trusted friend or counselor.
- Don't pretend to be okay when you're not. Let yourself feel.

You are not weak for having emotions. You are human.

3. Mental Self-Love

Your mind needs rest and stimulation both. Mental self-love includes anything that keeps your thoughts calm and focused.

Examples:

- Read a good book that inspires you.

- Learn something new: a language, a skill, or a hobby.
- Limit overthinking by practicing mindfulness or deep breathing.
- Take a break from screens.

Your thoughts shape your day. So mental care means feeding your mind with healthy, positive, and calming inputs.

4. Spiritual Self-Love

You don't have to be religious to care for your spirit. Spiritual self-love is about connecting to something bigger than yourself. It's about finding peace within.

Simple practices:

- Sit in silence and just breathe.
- Go for a walk in nature without distractions.
- Pray, meditate, or read spiritual texts.
- Reflect on your values and life purpose.

Your soul also needs attention. Don't forget to nourish it.

Self-Love Activity Planner

Let's make this practical. Below is a table to help you plan self-love across all four areas:

Pillar	Activity	Frequency
Vitality (Physical Self-Love)	Walk for 30 minutes	5 days a week
Resonance (Emotional Self-Love)	Journal your feelings	Daily
Clarity (Mental Self-Love)	Read one chapter of a book	4 days a week

Essence (Spiritual Self-Love)	Meditate for 10 minutes	Every morning
Expression (Creative & Hobby Self-Love)	Paint or sketch	Twice a week
Connection (Relational Self-Love)	Call a loved one	Weekly
Alignment (Lifestyle & Purpose Self-Love)	Reflect on goals & priorities	Every Sunday

You can change the activities and frequencies according to your needs. The idea is to begin with small, doable actions.

Exercise: Designing Your Ideal Self-Love Plan

Take a notebook or digital note app and write down:

1. One activity under each category that you enjoy or want to try.
2. Decide how many times a week you'll do each one. Be realistic.
3. Add them to your daily or weekly planner.
4. At the end of each week, reflect:
    - What felt good?
    - What felt forced?
    - What do you want to change?

Self-love is not fixed. It changes with your life. Some weeks you'll need more sleep; other weeks you may need more silence. Be flexible and kind to yourself.

Guided Meditation: Connecting with Your Inner Self

Meditation doesn't need to be complicated. This is a simple 10-minute guided meditation to help you feel calm, centered, and connected to yourself.

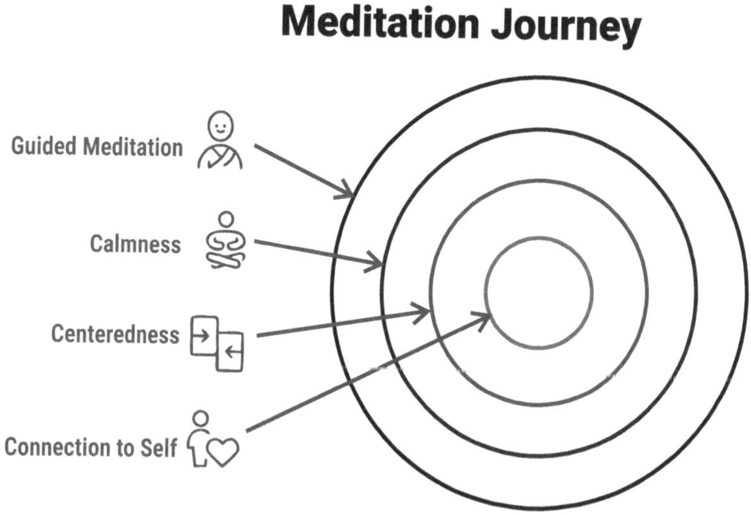

Try this once a day or whenever you feel lost or anxious.

1. Find a quiet space—your room, your balcony, or even your parked car.
2. Sit comfortably. Close your eyes. Breathe deeply—slow inhales and slow exhales.
3. Imagine a warm, golden light around your body, like sunlight gently hugging you.

4. With each breath in, feel this light entering your chest, filling your heart with peace.
5. As you breathe out, imagine releasing stress, worry, or any heavy feeling.
6. Picture yourself standing in a peaceful place—maybe a beach, a mountain, or a garden.
7. Feel safe. You are held. You are protected.
8. Now ask gently: "What do I need right now?"
9. Don't think. Just feel. Let the answer come naturally—rest, love, connection, forgiveness?
10. Sit with that feeling. Let it stay in your heart.
11. Slowly, open your eyes and take that peace with you through the day.

You can even record these steps in your voice and listen to them daily. It's like giving your soul a gentle massage.

How Self-Love Changes You

When you practice self-love regularly:

- Your mood improves.
- Your energy increases.
- You start saying yes to things that matter.
- You stop chasing people or things that drain you.
- You start trusting your inner voice.

Self-love is the quiet revolution. It's how you take your power back.

And the truth is—you don't have to earn it. You don't need to 'deserve' it. You are allowed to take care of yourself—always.

Self-Love Is Not Selfish

This is very important to understand. Society sometimes makes us believe that taking time for ourselves is selfish or lazy. But think about it:

- Can you pour from an empty cup?
- Can you support others if you are exhausted or unhappy?

You matter. Your needs matter. Your rest matters.

If you've spent your life putting everyone else first, it may feel strange to take care of yourself. But it's okay. It's never too late to start.

Start small:

- Take a long bath.
- Sleep an extra hour.
- Say no without explaining.
- Eat something that makes you smile.
- Go outside and breathe fresh air.

These small acts, repeated daily, become powerful habits.

Common Myths About Self-Love

Let's clear some doubts many people have:

Myth 1: I don't have time for self-love.

Reality: Even 5–10 minutes a day can make a difference. It's about consistency, not duration.

Myth 2: Self-love is expensive.

Reality: Most of the best self-love practices are free—walking, deep breathing, journaling, resting.

Myth 3: Self-love is only for people who are struggling.

Reality: Self-love is for everyone. It helps you avoid burnout and stay mentally and emotionally fit.

A Loving Reminder

You are not a machine. You are a living being with needs, feelings, and limits.

If you're tired, rest. If you're sad, cry. If you're overwhelmed, breathe. If you're lost, pause.

You don't have to do everything today. You don't have to be perfect.

Self-love is how you learn to be on your own side.

So today, take one small step—drink a glass of water mindfully, stretch your arms, close your eyes for a moment, or write one kind sentence to yourself.

You deserve it.

TIME TO THINK

1. **Which area of self-love (physical, emotional, mental, or spiritual) do you currently give the least attention to, and why do you think that is?**

2. **What's one simple, free activity you can add to your daily routine starting today to improve your self-love?**

3. **How would your life change if you truly believed that taking care of yourself is not selfish, but necessary?**

5
Chapter

Establishing Healthy Boundaries

"Love yourself unconditionally, just as you love those closest to you despite their faults."

~ Les Brown

Objective:

Learning to say NO and prioritizing self-love without guilt.

Understanding Boundaries and Their Importance

Boundaries are like invisible fences we create to protect our mental, emotional, and physical well-being. They help define where we end and where others begin. Just like a house needs walls to feel safe, we need boundaries to feel emotionally secure.

Imagine living in a house without doors—you wouldn't feel safe, would you? That's exactly what life feels like without boundaries. Anyone can walk in, make demands, hurt us, or take advantage of our time and energy. Setting boundaries isn't about keeping people out; it's about knowing who and what gets access to you, and on what terms.

Without boundaries:

- We feel emotionally drained and mentally exhausted.
- Our time gets hijacked by others' needs.
- Resentment builds up silently.
- Our self-worth takes a hit because we're constantly people-pleasing.

On the other hand, healthy boundaries:

- Improve the quality of our relationships.
- Allow us to prioritize self-love.
- Reduce stress.
- Build inner confidence and self-respect.

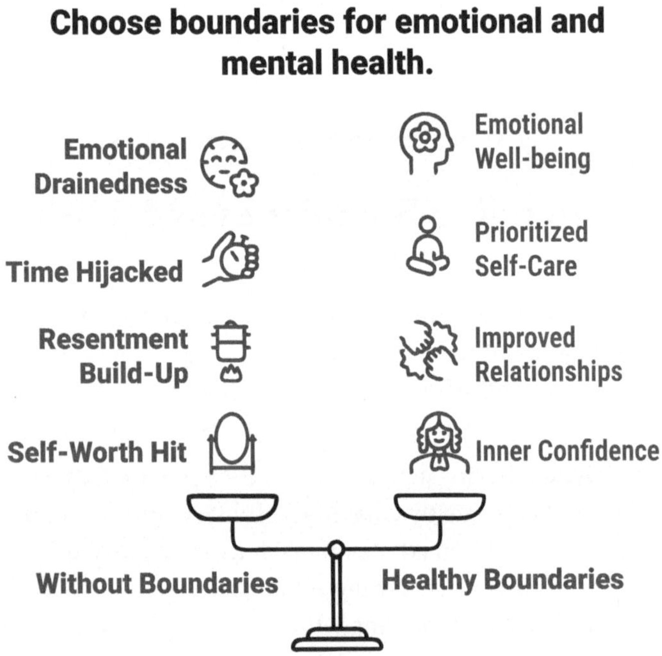

Boundaries aren't about being rude or selfish. They are about saying, "This is what I need to feel safe, respected, and happy."

Types of Boundaries

Understanding different types of boundaries helps us identify where we're most vulnerable and where we need the most protection:

1. **Emotional Boundaries**

   These protect your inner emotional world. If someone constantly manipulates your feelings, makes you feel guilty, or disregards how you feel, your emotional boundaries are being crossed.

2. **Time Boundaries**

   Everyone has the same 24 hours, but how we use them depends on the boundaries we set. Saying yes to every request leaves no time for yourself. Saying no respectfully is how you reclaim your hours.

3. **Physical Boundaries**

   This includes your need for personal space, touch, rest, and comfort. If someone invades your space or makes you uncomfortable physically, it's a sign your boundary needs reinforcement.

4. **Mental Boundaries**

   You're entitled to your thoughts, values, and beliefs. If someone constantly dismisses your opinions, tries to change your thinking without consent, or argues just to dominate, that's a red flag.

5. **Energetic Boundaries**

   These are invisible but powerful. Some people radiate positivity, while others constantly complain, criticize, or drain your vibe. You don't have to absorb anyone's energy—you can learn to protect your own.

Exercise: Identifying Energy Drainers

Grab a notebook and reflect deeply.

- **Who or what drains your energy the most?** Think of people, habits, work tasks, or places.
- **How do these interactions make you feel—tense, anxious, tired, small?**
- **What specific boundaries can you put in place?** Is it limiting time with someone? Saying no to events?
- **How can you communicate these boundaries without guilt or conflict?** Practice scripting your response kindly yet firmly.

Action Step: Pick one energy drainer and set a boundary around it this week. Maybe it's not replying to messages instantly or stepping away from someone who interrupts your peace. Track how it makes you feel.

Why Self-Love Requires Self-Protection

You cannot truly love yourself if you don't protect yourself. Love without protection is incomplete.

Many of us are raised to believe that putting others first is the right thing. While kindness is valuable, consistently ignoring your needs leads to emotional burnout. Protecting your energy isn't selfish—it's essential.

When you set healthy boundaries:

- You stop feeling like a doormat.
- You start respecting yourself.
- Others begin to treat you the way you treat yourself.

Healthy boundaries make your relationships more real. You show up as your honest self, not as someone faking happiness. And when people know your limits, they learn to value your presence.

Setting boundaries is not about building walls—it's about building clarity. It's saying, "This is where I end and where you begin."

Exercise: Creating a Personal Boundary Statement

Take a moment and write down your answers:

- **Emotional:** "I will not tolerate..." (e.g., people who dismiss my feelings)
- **Time:** "I will prioritize..." (e.g., my personal time and rest)
- **Physical:** "I am comfortable with..." (e.g., hugs only from close friends)
- **Mental:** "I have the right to my own opinions. I will not engage in..." (e.g., debates that feel toxic)
- **Energetic:** "I will protect my energy by..." (e.g., walking away from gossip or negativity)

Now, craft your Personal Boundary Statement. Example:

"I respect my time, emotions, and energy. I will no longer engage with people who drain my energy without reciprocation. I prioritize my well-being by saying no when necessary, without guilt. My needs matter, and I deserve to be treated with respect."

Action Step: Read your statement aloud every morning for a week. Let it become your daily reminder that you are allowed to protect your peace.

Affirmation Practice: Reinforcing Healthy Boundaries

Repeat these out loud, write them in your journal, or keep them in your phone:

- "I honor my needs and set healthy boundaries."
- "My time and energy are valuable."
- "I have the right to say no without feeling guilty."
- "I am worthy of relationships that respect my boundaries."
- "I protect my peace by choosing where to invest my energy."

Affirmations work best when repeated with belief and consistency. Speak to yourself the way you'd encourage a loved one.

Meditation: Shield of Protection

Let's build a mental space of safety and strength.

Steps:

1. Sit in a quiet space with no distractions.
2. Close your eyes and breathe slowly. Inhale calm, exhale tension.
3. Visualize a soft light forming around you. This is your protective shield.
4. With each breath, imagine it growing stronger and warmer. It blocks negativity and invites peace.

5. Picture someone or a situation where you often lose your boundary.
6. Visualize yourself calmly saying, "No." Imagine walking away with confidence and calm.
7. Repeat silently:
   - "I am protected. My energy is sacred."
   - "I give myself permission to set and maintain boundaries."
   - "I am safe, I am strong, I am in control of my space."
8. Stay here for a few more deep breaths.
9. Wiggle your fingers and toes. Gently open your eyes.
10. Carry this feeling of inner protection with you through the day.

Real-Life Tips to Strengthen Boundaries:

Try these simple changes:

- Don't over-explain when you say no. A short "I'm not available" is enough.
- Pause before committing. Buy yourself time by saying, "Let me check and get back to you."
- Use gentle but firm phrases: "I understand, but I can't take this on right now."
- Respect others' boundaries too. Healthy boundaries go both ways.

Bonus Thought: Boundaries Are the Bridges to Balance

Think of boundaries not as blocks, but as bridges—bridges that help you balance your needs with the world around you. They help you stay grounded, fulfilled, and in charge of your life.

Every time you honor your boundary; you teach others how to treat you. Every time you protect your peace; you strengthen your self-love.

Final Reminder:

You are not responsible for other people's happiness, but you are 100% responsible for protecting your peace.

Boundaries are a gift you give yourself—and they are the foundation of a balanced, fulfilling life.

Time To Think

1. **Where in your life do you currently feel most drained and what boundary, if set, could restore your peace?**

2. **Which type of boundary (emotional, time, physical, mental, energetic) do you struggle with the most and why?**

3. **How would your relationships change if you started honoring your personal boundary statement every day—without guilt?**

6
Chapter

Practicing Radical Self-Love

"Loving yourself isn't vanity. It's sanity."
~ Katrina Mayer

Objective:

To make self-love an unshakable priority in your daily life, not an optional luxury.

What is Radical Self-Love?

Radical self-love is not about indulgence. It's about intention. It's not a spa appointment or an impulsive day off. It's the unwavering choice to prioritize your own well-being—mentally, physically, emotionally, and spiritually, every single day.

Achieving Radical Self-Care

Neglecting Self
Ignoring personal well-being

Prioritize Needs
Recognize and address personal needs

Nurture Self
Take proactive steps for self-care

Cultivate Resilience
Improve overall quality of life

Empowered Self
Sustainable practice of self-love

Radical self-love means:

- You don't wait until you crash to rest.
- You don't seek permission to pause.
- You don't chase productivity to prove your worth.

You claim your space. You honor your needs. You live aligned.

This kind of care is an act of rebellion in a world that glorifies hustle and burnout. It's radical because it challenges cultural norms and reclaims self-worth from the claws of external validation.

Radical self-love is:

- A daily decision to choose yourself.
- A boundary-setting ritual.
- A declaration: I matter, and I act like it.

When practiced consistently, it transforms not only how you feel, but how you live, lead, and love.

Understanding the Depth of Radical Self-Love

Let's look deeper into how this differs from surface-level self-love. Here's a snapshot:

Casual Self-Love	Radical Self-Love
"I'll rest when I can."	"I build rest into my life."
A pamper session now and then	A sustainable, daily practice
Often used to recover from burnout	Used to prevent burnout altogether
Reactive to stress	Proactive in protection

Radical self-love doesn't wait for a breakdown. It prevents the breakdown. It's about resilience, clarity, and consistency. It doesn't whisper; it speaks boldly.

When you embrace it, you stop seeing self-love as a luxury. You see it as survival, sustainability, and soul nourishment.

It's waking up and checking in with your inner landscape before opening your inbox. It's making meals that love you back. It's choosing nourishing rest over numbing distractions. It's asking "What do I need?" before the day decides it for you.

It's courage. It's commitment. It's coming home to yourself, again and again.

Self-Love is Priority

Let's address the guilt.

Many of us have internalized the belief that caring for ourselves means we're being selfish or lazy. Especially if we're caregivers, professionals, leaders, or parents.

But this belief is a lie. A dangerous one.

The truth is:

- You can't give your best if you're always running on empty.
- Being available to everyone but yourself is not noble—it's unsustainable.
- Prioritizing your well-being is the opposite of selfishness. It's fundamental.

Think of yourself as a battery. If you don't recharge, you drain. Eventually, everything connected to you flickers too.

Radical self-love says:

- I don't wait until I collapse.
- I don't need a crisis to justify care.
- I am worth showing up for—daily.

And here's something deeper: modeling self-love creates a ripple. When others see you making your well-being non-negotiable, they feel empowered to do the same. You give silent permission. You become a living reminder that it's okay to pause, to say no, to rest.

You break cycles. You build new legacies.

Exercise 1: The Self-Love Reflection Grid (Deep Dive)

On a page or digital note, draw three columns labeled: **Physical, Emotional, and Mental.**

Physical Self-Love

- Do I sleep deeply and consistently for 7–9 hours?
- Am I eating nutrient-dense meals or comfort foods that leave me drained?

- Do I experience joyful movement or is exercise a punishment?
- Do I check in with how my body feels or just how it looks?

Emotional Self-Love

- Do I express my feelings, or suppress them?
- Who in my life supports my emotional growth?
- Do I have emotional outlets—journaling, therapy, art, etc.?
- How do I handle emotional triggers or discomfort?

Mental Self-Love

- Is my mind constantly overstimulated?
- Do I create space for quiet thinking or just react to noise?
- Am I protecting my attention from digital overwhelm?
- What mental habits uplift me—and which ones drain me?

Action: Choose one category where your answers felt weak. Write down 2 small changes you'll try this week. Make them easy and doable.

Insight: Is It Healing or Escaping?

A Netflix marathon feels like a break until it becomes avoidable. A glass of wine feels like comfort until it's masking pain. A social media scroll feels like a connection until you realize you feel emptier after.

There's a difference between healing and escaping.

Healing reconnects you. Escaping disconnects you.

Ask yourself:

- Is this choice soothing or avoiding?
- Am I facing what needs attention or dodging it?

- How do I feel after doing this activity: clearer or foggier?

Examples:

- Journaling: Healing.
- Emotional eating: Escaping.
- Talking with a trusted friend: Healing.
- Constant distraction with reels: Escaping.

List 3 habits you turn to when you're overwhelmed. Categorize them. Replace one escapist habit this week with something nurturing.

Bonus Insight: Healing isn't always soft. Sometimes it's uncomfortable. It looks like setting boundaries that upset people. Like sitting in silence instead of numbing with noise. Like asking for help instead of pretending you're fine. Don't confuse discomfort with doing it wrong. Sometimes, that's the clearest sign you're finally doing it right.

Exercise 2: Create Your Non-Negotiable Self-Love Blueprint

Habits stick when they have structure. Your self-love shouldn't rely on willpower—it should rely on rhythm.

DAILY CARE (15-45 minutes)

- Morning check-in: "How do I feel today?"
- Hydrate before coffee.
- 10-minute joyful movement or breathwork.
- Practice digital boundaries (no phone during meals).
- End the day with gratitude journaling or 5-minute meditation.

WEEKLY CARE (1-2 hours)

- Do a digital detox for one evening.
- Cook one nourishing meal with love.
- Clean a corner of your space that's been neglected.
- Schedule a "no agenda" walk or park visit.

MONTHLY CARE (2-4 hours)

- Go on a solo artist date: museum, coffee, hike, etc.
- Do a feelings inventory: What do I need more of? Less of?
- Detox one draining commitment.
- Try something new—class, book, or recipe.

Your Task: Use this template to create your version. Write it somewhere visible: a planner, phone wallpaper, or fridge magnet. Revisit it weekly.

Extra Tip: Tie your self-love moments to anchors. For example, do a breathing practice right after brushing your teeth. Or journal while your tea steeps. Anchoring habits makes them easier to repeat.

Words to Live By: Daily Self-Love Affirmations

Words aren't just sounds—they're spells. Speak gently to yourself until you believe in your own worth.

Repeat daily:

- "I am allowed to rest without guilt."
- "Caring for myself is an act of love, not selfishness."
- "I deserve ease, joy, and healing."
- "I am not behind. I am growing at my own pace."

- "Self-love is how I say: I am enough."

Practice: Record your favorite affirmation and play it every morning. Bonus: Say it while looking in the mirror.

Try writing new ones too. Let them come from your own truth:

- "I trust the timing of my healing."
- "My worth is not measured by my output."
- "Rest is a sacred act."

Guided Meditation: 5-Minute Full Body Check-In

This practice reconnects you with your body's wisdom.

1. Sit upright or lie down.
2. Close your eyes. Breathe in through your nose for 4 counts, hold for 4, and exhale for 6.
3. Feel your feet grounding. Wiggle your toes. Release any tension.
4. Move awareness to your calves, knees, and thighs. Soften these areas.
5. Bring awareness to your belly. Notice if you're holding it tight—breathe into it.
6. Check your chest and heart space. Feel the rhythm.
7. Unclench your jaw. Let your shoulders drop.
8. Place a hand on your heart. Say: "I am safe at this moment."
9. Take three deep breaths and smile gently.

Use this practice: Before work meetings, after conflicts, or to start your day grounded.

Optional Extension: Pair this with a soothing sound or music playlist. Let it become a ritual you look forward to. Name this moment. Claim it as your reset.

Real-Life Practices: Self-Love in Action

Let's bring this off the page and into real life:

- **Say no without explaining.** No is a full sentence.
- **Take guilt-free breaks** when tired—don't wait for permission.
- **Unfollow or mute** accounts that make you feel small.
- **Pause before reacting.** Responding is power.
- **Create tech-free zones** in your home or day.
- **Celebrate small wins.** Rest is a reward, not only for giant achievements.
- **Walk slower.** Eat slower. Breathe deeper. Let slowness be sacred.
- **Create an "Emergency Self-Love Kit."** Include a favorite book, playlist, cozy socks, snacks, a journal, and a reminder letter from your best self.

Final Thoughts: Make Self-Love a Non-Negotiable Lifestyle

Radical self-love is not a checklist. It's not a weekend luxury. It's a promise to yourself.

You're not required to earn rest. You don't have to prove burnout to be worthy of healing. You are allowed to choose yourself, daily, and out loud.

The more you honor your needs, the more you become a lighthouse not only lighting your path but illuminating the way for others too.

Because when you rise, others rise with you.

Your self-love becomes a legacy.

Time To Think

1. **Which current self-love habit in your life feels more like an escape than true healing and what small shift can you make this week to transform it into something nourishing?**

2. **If you truly believed resting is as important as working, how would your thoughts or routine change?**

3. **What is one "no" you find hard to say but would make you feel lighter if you did?**

7
Chapter

Living Authentically and Fearlessly

"When you recover or discover something that nourishes your soul and brings joy, care enough about yourself to make room for it in your life."

~ Jean Shinoda Bolen

Objective:

Embracing your true self unapologetically.

What Does It Mean to Live Authentically?

Living authentically means living in alignment with who you truly are—beneath the expectations, labels, and roles society places on you. It's not about rebelling or rejecting everything around you. Rather, it's about embracing what feels true within you and expressing it courageously, even when it's not easy.

To live authentically:

- You accept yourself fully—flaws, fears, quirks, strengths, and all.

- You stop performing for approval and start showing up as you.
- You no longer mold yourself to be what others want—you reclaim your right to be your whole, unfiltered self.
- You live from your values and passions instead of fear and obligation.
- You recognize that imperfections are not weaknesses—they are part of your truth.

Authenticity doesn't mean perfection. It means honesty. It means letting go of the stories you've been told and writing your own. It's the permission you give yourself to be real in a world that rewards the filtered and the polished. Being authentic is not loud or attention-seeking; it's quietly powerful. It's living with integrity—not just in what you do, but in who you are.

The Cycle of Authenticity

The journey to authenticity isn't always straightforward. It requires shedding layers that no longer serve us and stepping into our truth, even when it feels uncomfortable. But with each honest step, we grow lighter, stronger, and freer.

The Fear That Holds Us Back

We are often taught, directly or indirectly, to hide parts of ourselves. Perhaps you've heard statements like:

- "Don't speak too loudly."
- "Be more like them."
- "You can't wear that."
- "Don't dream so big."

These voices begin as whispers and become internal beliefs: I'm too much, I'm not enough, I have to earn love, I need to be perfect to be accepted.

Living authentically requires recognizing these inherited beliefs and gently unlearning them. It means asking: *Whose voice is this? Is this truly mine?*

You cannot be free while living according to someone else's script. The fear of not fitting in or being misunderstood often keeps us locked in roles we never chose. But here's the truth: the right people will celebrate your authenticity. The wrong ones will fall away, and that's okay.

Fear is natural, but it doesn't have to be the driver. When you challenge your fear with truth, something powerful happens: you begin to reclaim your life.

Exercise: Who Am I Without Fear?

Imagine a world where there's no fear of judgment, failure, or rejection. Picture yourself in that world.

Now ask:

- If no one could criticize me, how would I speak?
- What would I wear if I wasn't worried about fitting in?
- What truths would I finally allow myself to say aloud?
- What would I create, explore, or express?

Take time with this exercise. Write freely. Let your answers surprise you. Often, the answers reveal our truest longings—the dreams buried beneath self-protection.

Action Step: Identify one small, bold action to take this week that reflects the answers above. It could be as simple as wearing bold colors, introducing yourself with pride, saying no without guilt, or finally starting that passion project. These small actions become the building blocks of a life lived fully and fearlessly.

Understanding the Masks We Wear

We all wear masks. We put on the "responsible one," the "pleaser," the "strong one," or the "perfect parent" mask. These roles may have protected us, earned us praise, or helped us survive difficult environments.

But over time, these masks become heavy.

When we're always performing, we start to forget who we really are.

Start noticing where in your life you feel like you're acting.

- Do you pretend to agree when you don't?
- Do you hide your dreams because they feel "unrealistic"?
- Do you downplay your emotions to avoid discomfort?

Living authentically means removing these layers. One by one. Gently. Until what's left is you.

Not a version of you that's polished for approval—but the raw, radiant, honest version that has been waiting to be seen.

Give yourself grace through this unmasking process. Some masks are tied to safety. You don't have to rip them off. You can lay them down, softly, when you're ready.

Insight: The Power of Authenticity

Authenticity is magnetic. When you show up as your real self:

- Your confidence grows because you're not wasting energy hiding or pretending.
- You attract people who truly see you, not your mask.
- Your decisions become clearer because they're guided by inner truth, not outer pressure.
- You stop seeking permission to be happy. You become the source of your own validation.
- You feel lighter. There's peace in no longer hiding.

Authentic people also create ripple effects. When you live from your truth, you give silent permission to others to do the same. You become a mirror of possibility.

Reflection: Recall a moment in your life when you felt completely yourself. Who were you with? What were you doing? How did it feel in your body and spirit?

Write about how you can invite more of that feeling into your life today.

Exercise: Writing Your Personal Manifesto

A personal manifesto is your soul's declaration. It's a promise to yourself—a bold, clear articulation of who you are and how you choose to live.

Step 1: Define Your Core Values

Reflect on what matters deeply to you. Some examples include:

- Honesty
- Kindness
- Freedom
- Adventure
- Authenticity
- Creativity
- Courage

Write down your top 3–5 core values.

Step 2: Express How You Will Honor Them

Write short, powerful statements of how you'll embody these values. Examples:

- "I will speak truthfully, even when it feels scary."
- "I will protect my energy and say no without guilt."
- "I will follow my creative instincts, not the crowd."

Step 3: Declare Your Self-Love Commitment

This is the heart of your manifesto. How will you treat yourself? How will you commit to being YOU, even when it's uncomfortable?

Example Manifesto:

"I am committed to living my truth. I will not apologize for who I am. I honor my voice, my feelings, and my dreams. I release fear, self-doubt, and the need for approval. I am free to be my true self, and I embrace my journey with courage and love."

Action Step: Write your own manifesto and read it aloud each morning. Let it anchor your day in authenticity.

Authentic Expression in Daily Life

Authenticity isn't just about the big choices. It's also in the small daily moments:

- Saying no when something doesn't align.
- Letting yourself cry when you're sad.
- Laughing loudly when you're joyful.
- Asking for what you need without shame.
- Saying "I don't know" without guilt.

These are not just habits—they are acts of liberation.

Living authentically is not about being perfect; it's about being present. It's about telling the truth when it matters most, even if your voice shakes.

Action: What's one area where you usually hide or shrink? Decide on a single, simple way to show up more honestly in that space this week.

Affirmation Practice: Embracing Your True Self

Affirmations are not magic spells. They are truths you choose to speak until your mind and heart believe them again.

Repeat these daily:

- "I am free to be my true self."
- "I release the need for approval. I am enough."
- "I trust my inner voice and honor my authenticity."

- "My uniqueness is my greatest strength."
- "I choose authenticity over perfection."

Practice: Pick the one that stirs something in you. Write it in your journal daily. Say it aloud. Let it become your compass.

Meditation: Meeting Your Higher Self

This guided visualization helps you connect with the truest, most empowered version of yourself.

1. Find a quiet place. Sit comfortably.
2. Close your eyes. Take deep breaths.
3. Picture a peaceful path unfolding before you. This is your path to truth.
4. As you walk, feel yourself shedding layers—fear, doubt, masks.
5. Ahead, you see your Higher Self—glowing with confidence and ease.
6. Approach with reverence. Observe their presence. Their posture. Their peace.
7. Ask: "What do you want me to remember?"
8. Listen. Feel. Receive.
9. Embrace your Higher Self.
10. Affirm: "I carry my Higher Self within me always."
11. Slowly return to your body. Open your eyes.

Reflection: Journal the message you received. How can you honor this guidance today?

Living Authentically as a Daily Practice

Living authentically isn't a one-time declaration. It's a practice—a choice you make again and again.

Some days you'll feel bold. Other days you'll feel vulnerable.

But every day is an invitation to return to your truth.

- When you're afraid, pause and ask: What would my true self do here?
- When you feel lost, return to your values.
- When you feel pressured to conform, breathe and remember your manifesto.

You're not here to be liked by everyone. You're here to be YOU.

Final Invitation: Reclaim Your Voice

Authentic living is the deepest form of freedom.

You stop chasing someone else's definition of success. You stop silencing your needs and dreams. You become the author of your own story.

Let this chapter be your permission slip. To stop editing yourself. To speak. To move. To choose.

Your life is not a performance. It's a creation.

And the most beautiful thing you can ever create is a life that feels like home.

TIME TO THINK

1. **What is one small thing you can do this week to be more yourself?**

____

____

____

____

____

2. **Do you hide your true feelings or thoughts sometimes? When? How can you share a little more honestly?**

____

____

____

____

____

3. **If no one would judge you, what would you like to say or do?**

____

____

____

____

____

8

Chapter

Embracing Self-Actualization and Inner Peace

"To fall in love with yourself is the first secret to happiness."

~ Robert Morley

Objective:

Reaching a state of deep self-love and alignment with your purpose.

What is Self-Actualization?

Self-actualization is the process of realizing and fulfilling your highest potential. It is the moment when you embrace who you truly are, live in alignment with your purpose, and experience profound inner peace.

The philosopher Abraham Maslow first introduced self-actualization as the pinnacle of human development, where people realize their fullest potential and live authentically. Yet, in practical terms, self-actualization transcends any checklist. It is a dynamic state of inner clarity and acceptance. This process awakens when you begin to honor your deepest desires and values, even when they challenge the norms around you.

But what does this really mean on a deeper level?

Self-actualization is not simply achieving external success or ticking off goals. It's about uncovering the essence of who you are beneath all societal conditioning and expectations. Imagine peeling back layers of doubts, fears, and limiting beliefs to reveal your authentic self—the person you were born to be.

It is a sacred journey inward, a conscious awakening to your true nature. When self-actualized, you act from a place of integrity, creativity, and freedom. Your choices align with your deepest values rather than external pressures or transient desires.

This state is marked by an inner harmony where your thoughts, emotions, and actions flow together effortlessly. You begin to experience life not as a series of challenges to overcome but as a continuous unfolding of growth and joy.

Signs of Self-Actualization

Recognizing when you are stepping into self-actualization can sometimes feel elusive. It's often a subtle transformation rather than a dramatic event. Here are some clear signs that you are embracing your highest self:

- **A Deep Sense of Fulfillment and Inner Contentment:** You feel at peace with yourself and your life, regardless of circumstances. This contentment is not dependent on external validation but arises from within.
- **Confidence in Your Own Worth Without Seeking External Validation:** You no longer require others' approval to feel good about yourself. Your sense of worth is intrinsic and unwavering.
- **Living in Alignment With Your Values, Passions, and Purpose:** Your daily actions and choices reflect what matters most to you. You pursue what ignites your soul rather than what society tells you to want.
- **Letting Go of Fear, Self-Doubt, and Unnecessary Worries:** You no longer let fear dictate your decisions. Self-doubt may appear occasionally, but it doesn't hold power over you.
- **Cultivating Peace and Joy in Everyday Moments:** You find beauty and gratitude in the small things—a warm cup of tea, a smile from a stranger, the sound of birds. These simple moments ground you in joy.

This state of being is not static. It grows deeper over time as you continue to nurture yourself and evolve.

Exercise: Designing Your Ideal Life

To create a life that aligns with your deepest self, take a moment to reflect deeply and intentionally:

1. **Imagine Your Ideal Self-Loving Life:**

   Close your eyes and picture your ideal day in vivid detail. Where are you? What are you doing? Who is with you? What emotions fill your heart? Describe the environment around you—the sounds, sights, smells, and sensations.

2. **What Habits, Relationships, and Activities Contribute to This Version of You?**

   Consider what practices, rituals, or hobbies make you feel nourished and alive. What kind of people surround you? How do these relationships support your growth and authenticity?

3. **What Obstacles Are Currently Preventing You From Living This Way?**

   Be honest with yourself about fears, limiting beliefs, time constraints, or negative influences holding you back. Awareness is the first step toward change.

4. **What Small Steps Can You Take Today to Align With This Vision?**

   Identify realistic, manageable actions that can shift your life closer to this ideal. Even tiny changes compound over time to create powerful transformation.

Action Step: Write a Letter From Your Future Self

Write a heartfelt letter from your future self-thanking you for taking the courageous steps toward living your best life. Imagine how your life has transformed because of the choices you made, the habits you adopted, and the love you cultivated.

Describe the peace you now carry, the clarity you've gained, and the joy you experience daily. Let this letter be a source of motivation and reassurance, reminding you that the future you desire is within reach.

Insight: The Journey Never Ends

One of the most beautiful truths about self-love and self-actualization is that it is an ongoing process. It is not a destination to arrive at but a lifelong unfolding.

There is no "final destination." Life is a continuous cycle of learning, growing, and embracing change. Each day offers new opportunities to deepen your self-awareness and reconnect with your purpose.

As you accept and love yourself more fully, you naturally attract peace, joy, and meaningful experiences into your life. This ripple effect touches every area—from relationships to career to health.

Remember that setbacks or moments of doubt are natural. They do not signal failure but invite you to show yourself greater compassion and patience.

Reflection: Your Personal Growth Milestones

Take time to reflect on how far you have already come on your journey.

- What personal growth milestones have you achieved?
- How have you changed for the better over the years?
- What lessons have shaped your character and resilience?

Celebrate these wins, big or small, as markers of your evolving self.

Exercise: The Gratitude Reflection

Gratitude plays a central role in cultivating self-actualization because it shifts your focus toward the abundance and beauty already present in your life.

1. **Write Down 10 Things You Are Grateful for About Yourself:**

   Think beyond superficial traits and include your strengths, resilience, moments of courage, and the ways you've grown emotionally and spiritually.

2. **Reflect on How Far You've Come:**

   Recall your biggest personal growth moments. What challenges did you overcome? What new perspectives have you gained?

3. **Write a Gratitude Letter to Yourself:**

   Express appreciation for the efforts you've made to become the person you are today. Recognize the love and determination that fueled your transformation.

Action Step: Keep a Gratitude Journal

Commit to writing three things you appreciate about yourself every night before bed. Over time, this practice rewires your mind to notice and celebrate your worth and growth regularly.

Affirmation Practice: Embracing Inner Peace

Affirmations are powerful tools to reprogram your subconscious mind and cultivate a positive inner dialogue.

Repeat these affirmations daily with intention and belief:

- "I am whole, I am enough, I am love."
- "I trust my journey and embrace my growth."
- "My life unfolds beautifully in alignment with my purpose."
- "I find peace in who I am and where I am."
- "I am grateful for all that I am and all that I am becoming."

Feel the energy of each statement as you say it aloud, especially when looking at yourself in the mirror. Over time, these affirmations become a natural part of your thinking, helping you stay centered.

Practice: Morning Mirror Affirmation Ritual

Spend five minutes every morning speaking these affirmations to yourself in front of a mirror. Look directly into your eyes and speak with conviction and kindness. This ritual fosters self-love and confidence that carries you through the day.

Meditation: A Journey to Your Future Self

This powerful visualization meditation connects you to your highest potential and inner wisdom.

1. Find a quiet and peaceful place where you won't be disturbed. Sit comfortably and close your eyes.
2. Take deep, calming breaths: inhale through your nose for four counts, hold for four counts, and exhale slowly for six counts. Repeat this breathing pattern several times until you feel relaxed.
3. Visualize yourself walking down a beautiful path. This path represents your personal journey to self-actualization.
4. Ahead, you see your future self standing confidently. This version of you embodies deep self-love, wisdom, and inner peace.
5. Observe their presence carefully. How do they look? What kind of energy do they radiate? How do they carry themselves?
6. Approach your future self and ask these questions:
    - "What wisdom do you have for me?"
    - "What do I need to focus on right now?"
    - "How can I embody my highest potential?"
7. Listen attentively to their message. Allow their guidance to fill your heart with reassurance and strength.
8. Express gratitude to your future self. Let them know you are ready to step into your highest potential.
9. Slowly bring your awareness back to the present moment. Wiggle your fingers and toes, take a deep breath, and open your eyes.

10. Journal about your experience. Write down any insights, emotions, or messages you received.

Practice: Weekly Future Self Meditation

Repeat this meditation once a week to strengthen your connection to your highest self and align your actions with your purpose.

Additional Reflections on Embracing Self-Actualization

Self-actualization invites us to release the constant striving and perfectionism that often hold us back. Instead, it asks us to cultivate presence, patience, and acceptance.

It's important to understand that reaching this state doesn't mean life becomes free of challenges. Rather, you develop a new relationship with difficulties—viewing them as catalysts for growth rather than threats to your peace.

Another powerful aspect is the recognition of interconnectedness. As you embrace your authentic self, you become more compassionate and understanding toward others. You realize that everyone is on their own journey, facing their own struggles, and seeking their own peace.

Living With Intention: Daily Practices to Nurture Your Highest Self

To support your ongoing journey toward self-actualization and inner peace, consider weaving these daily practices into your routine:

- **Mindful Breathing:** Take intentional pauses during the day to focus on your breath. This anchors you in the present and calms your nervous system.

- **Journaling:** Reflect each day on your experiences, emotions, and insights. Writing clarifies your thoughts and deepens self-awareness.
- **Acts of Kindness:** Practice kindness toward yourself and others. Small acts—smiling, helping, listening—foster connection and joy.
- **Setting Boundaries:** Honor your energy and time by saying no to what drains you and yes to what nurtures you.
- **Creative Expression:** Engage in creative activities that bring you joy and help you express your inner world.

Final Thought: Embrace the Journey

Remember, self-actualization is a lifelong adventure; a sacred dance between self-discovery and self-love. There will be moments of clarity and moments of confusion, but every step brings you closer to the peace and authenticity that are your true nature.

Welcome this journey with openness and grace. Your highest self is not a distant dream but a present reality waiting for you to embrace.

TIME TO THINK

1. **What small things make you feel happy and peaceful inside right now?**

2. **What fears or worries stop you from being your true self?**

3. **Imagine your best future self: the person who feels peaceful, confident, and happy. What is one message or advice that future you would give to your present self?**

Final Thoughts & Commitment to Self-Love

"If you have the ability to love, love yourself first."
~ Charles Bukowski

Committing to Lifelong Self-Love

Your journey to self-love doesn't end here—it is something you carry with you every day for the rest of your life. Self-love is not a one-time achievement or a final destination you reach; it is a continuous process of growth, acceptance, and kindness towards yourself. Some days will be easier than others. There will be times when self-doubt, fear, or negativity may sneak in and make you question your worth. That's completely normal and part of being human.

What matters most is how you respond to those moments. Instead of giving in to harsh self-judgment, remind yourself that self-love means progress, not perfection. It means being patient and gentle with yourself as you learn and grow. It means recognizing your strengths, forgiving your mistakes, and choosing to treat yourself with the same compassion you would offer a dear friend.

Self-love helps you build resilience so you can face life's challenges with confidence and grace. It gives you the courage to set healthy boundaries, say "no" when you need to, and put your well-being first without guilt. When you love yourself deeply, you begin to attract more peace, joy, and meaningful relationships into your life.

By signing the contract given on the next page, you are making a powerful and lifelong promise to prioritize your happiness and health. You are choosing to honor your feelings, respect your limits, and embrace your unique journey with an open heart. This commitment is your foundation for a life filled with purpose, fulfillment, and true inner peace.

SELF-LOVE CONTRACT

I, [Your Name], commit to loving, honoring, and accepting myself unconditionally.

I pledge to:

1. Treat myself with kindness, compassion, and respect.
2. Prioritize my mental, emotional, and physical well-being.
3. Forgive myself for past mistakes and allow myself to grow.
4. Set and maintain healthy boundaries without guilt.
5. Embrace my uniqueness and live authentically.
6. Let go of negative self-talk and replace it with self-empowering thoughts.
7. Celebrate my achievements and be proud of who I am.
8. Invest in relationships that uplift and support me.
9. Release comparison and recognize my intrinsic worth.
10. Choose self-love, even when it feels difficult.

Signed: ________________

Date: __________________

Action Step: Read this contract every morning as a reminder of your commitment to yourself.

DAILY SELF-LOVE CHECKLIST

To maintain progress, integrate these small self-love habits into your daily routine:

- ✓ **Morning Affirmations:** Start your day by affirming your worth (e.g., "I am enough," "I love and accept myself.").
- ✓ **Mindful Breathing:** Take deep breaths and center yourself in the present moment.
- ✓ **Gratitude Practice:** Write down three things you love about yourself.
- ✓ **Healthy Boundaries:** Say no when needed and protect your energy.
- ✓ **Self-Love Ritual:** Engage in an activity that nourishes your mind, body, or soul.
- ✓ **Journaling:** Reflect on your emotions and celebrate your wins.
- ✓ **Movement:** Stretch, dance, walk, or exercise—move your body with love.
- ✓ **Unplug & Recharge:** Take breaks from screens and social media to reconnect with yourself.
- ✓ **Evening Reflection:** End your day by acknowledging your progress and practicing self-compassion.
- ✓ **Positive Connection:** Reach out to someone who uplifts you or shares a kind word with yourself.

- ✓ **Nourishing Food & Hydration:** Choose foods and drinks that fuel your body gently and mindfully.
- ✓ **Acts of Kindness:** Do something small for yourself or others that brings joy and connection.

Action Step: Customize this checklist based on what works best for you. Keep it visible and make self-love a daily habit.

Additional Resources for Continued Growth

Books:

- *The Gifts of Imperfection* – Brené Brown
- *Radical Self-Love* – Gala Darling
- *You Can Heal Your Life* – Louise Hay
- *The Untethered Soul* – Michael A. Singer
- *Atomic Habits* – James Clear (great for building lasting self-love habits)

Podcasts:

- *The Self-Love Fix*
- *Unlocking Us* – Brené Brown
- *The Lavendaire Lifestyle*
- *On Purpose* – Jay Shetty

YouTube Channels for Self-Love & Growth:

- Lavendaire
- Mel Robbins

- SuperSoul Sunday (Oprah Winfrey)
- School of Greatness (Lewis Howes)

Self-Love Tools:

- **Self-Love Journal:** Track your affirmations, progress, and reflections.
- **Vision Board:** Visualize your self-love journey and future goals.
- **Meditation Apps:** Insight Timer, Headspace, or Calm for guided mindfulness practices.

Action Step: Explore at least one new resource this week that resonates with you and supports your journey.

Your Journey Continues

Self-love is not a one-time goal—it's a lifelong journey filled with ups and downs, lessons and victories. There will be days when you feel uncertain, days when old doubts creep back in. But there will also be moments of pure joy, deep clarity, and powerful transformation. Let those moments guide you.

Be gentle with yourself. You are evolving every single day, and there is no rush to be perfect. You are not behind. You are exactly where you need to be.

Each small act of love, each mindful breath, and every time you choose yourself over fear—you are rewriting your story.

You already have everything within you to create a life rooted in love, peace, and purpose. You are whole. You are worthy. You are enough. And you are deeply loved—just as you are.

- **Final Affirmation:**

  "I am always growing, always evolving, and always worthy of love."

CONCLUSION: BECOMING LOVE ITSELF

Living with Love & Purpose

Self-love is not just a private journey—it's a powerful energy that extends beyond you. When you truly embrace who you are, that love overflows into your actions, your words, and your relationships. It becomes your presence.

You begin to radiate love, and others feel it. This is how self-love becomes world-changing: not through grand gestures, but through consistent, intentional living. Your light becomes a guide for others still searching for theirs.

Here's how you can continue living with deep love and purpose:

- **Lead by Example:** Be the mirror of self-love. Respect your time, protect your energy, and show that it's okay to choose yourself first.
- **Spread Kindness:** Every kind word and action plants a seed of hope. Let your love show in small ways—smiles, support, or silent prayers.
- **Empower Others:** Your journey has value. Share your struggles and lessons—it may be the message someone else needs to hear today.
- **Live with Gratitude:** Love grows where gratitude lives. Take time to be thankful for your body, mind, journey, and the people who walk it with you.

- **Pursue Your Passions:** Your passions aren't random; they are whispers from your soul. By following them, you give others permission to do the same.
- Stay Present: Love is now. Let go of the past, stop chasing the future. Just be. Connect, listen, and breathe.
- **Forgive and Release:** Holding pain only binds you. Set yourself free through forgiveness—not to forget, but to rise above.

Action Step: Choose one of these practices and commit to it daily. Journal how it shifts your inner peace, relationships, and sense of purpose.

It's Time to Shine

To the beautiful soul reading this:

You are enough. You have always been enough, and you always will be.

This journey of self-love is one of courage, transformation, and deep healing. There will be days when doubts creep in, when the world feels heavy, and when you may question your worth. In those moments, remember:

- You are worthy, simply because you exist.
- You are love, and love flows within and around you.
- You are evolving every day—embrace the process.
- Your imperfections make you human, and your self-acceptance makes you powerful.
- The love you seek has always been within you.

This is not the end of your journey—it is only the beginning. Carry forward everything you've learned in this workbook, revisit the exercises when needed, and remind yourself that you are your greatest source of love.

You've just gone through almost a Wikipedia of how to build deep self-love—a step-by-step guide filled with insights, tools, and real talk. Now you have two choices:

1. You can take everything you've learned here and walk the path on your own

Or

2. If you have questions, need clarity, or simply want guidance on a particular part of this journey, I'm just one message away.

Book a 1-1 meeting or connect with me at:

support@prettykapoor.com

I'd love to hear your story. Let's grow together. You are becoming love itself, and the world is brighter because of you.

One Final Affirmation:

"I am love. I radiate love. I receive love."

This workbook is your guide, but your heart is the real teacher.

Trust it. Love it. Become it.

For more resources, visit:

http://www.prettykapoor.com/

With love and gratitude,

Preeti Kapoor